HOWEVER AND WHEREVER WE ARE

However
and Wherever
We Are

Poems from
Persea's First Fifty Years

A Karen & Michael Braziller Book
PERSEA BOOKS / NEW YORK

Introduction and compilation copyright © 2025 by Persea Books, Inc.

Because this page cannot legibly accommodate all copyright credits, pages 75–78 shall constitute an extension of the copyright page.

All rights reserved. No part of this publication may be reproduced or transmitted in any form or by any means, electronic or mechanical, including photocopy, audio recording, or any information storage and retrieval system, without prior permission in writing from the publisher. Request for permission or for information should be addressed to the publisher:

Persea Books, Inc.
90 Broad Street
New York, New York 10004

Library of Congress Control Number: 2025931310

Book design and composition by Rita Skingle
Typeset in Giovanni Std
Manufactured in the United States of America
Printed on acid-free paper

Contents

Introduction   vii

The Film / KATE NORTHROP   3

In Preparation / ELIZABETH BRADFIELD   4

from Odd to Anne Moffo / WAYNE KOESTENBAUM   5

On Living / NAZIM HIKMET   6

[Cut buds bloom awhile in a water glass] / SARA WAINSCOTT   9

Invocation / CAREY SALERNO   10

Bioluminescence / MICHAEL WHITE   11

She Ties My Bowtie / GABRIELLE CALVOCORESSI   12

[Take / for joy's sake / from these hands of mine] /
    OSIP MANDELSTAM   13

Runaway Bride / ALLISON SEAY   14

Two Drafts Written After a Fight / ALEXANDRA TEAGUE   15

A Difficult System / KIMBERLY GREY   16

Marriage / LAURA CRONK   17

[As the weather warms] / GARY YOUNG   18

Some History of Field Work / CHRISTOPHER SALERNO   19

Tornados / THYLIAS MOSS   20

Ritual X.: The Evening Pair of Ales / PAUL BLACKBURN   21

Museum of Science and History / SHANE MCCRAE   22

N'Jadaka's Appeal / JUBIA ARRIOLA-HEADLEY   23

Today Is Friday / RAMON GUTHRIE   24

Part of Eve's Discussion / MARIE HOWE   26

O / SIDNEY WADE   27

Raw Bar / RANDY BLASING   28

Ode on My Episiotomy / KIMBERLY JOHNSON   29

Nonsomnolent / EMILY VAN KLEY   30

Meditations in an Emergency / CAMERON AWKWARD-RICH   32

from A Language of Hemophilia / Tom Andrews 33

What I Would Ask You / Sarah Matthes 34

Assisi / Paul Celan 35

Continuum / Mitchell L. H. Douglas 36

The Central Virginia Training Center / Molly McCully Brown 37

Torsion / Susannah Nevison 39

What Silence Equals / Tory Dent 40

Ode to Flint, Michigan, Five Years, Three Months, Ten Days
after the Water Crisis Began / Sarah Carson 42

Milwaukee, 1968 / Valencia Robin 44

Rain at Reading / Rachel Wetzsteon 45

Song / Randall Mann 46

Jocks / Caki Wilkinson 47

Team / Aaron Belz 48

I Am Not from the Philippines / Sarah Gambito 49

3 October / Amy Newman 50

Road Scatter / Sandra Meek 51

The Stork / Cynthia Marie Hoffman 52

You Can Always Freeze Your Eggs / Rachel Galvin 54

Black Line / Anne Marie Macari 55

Xī'ān Nocturne with Jasmine and Pears / Anni Liu 56

Anyway / James Richardson 57

Children Walk on Chairs to Cross a Flooded Schoolyard /
Patrick Rosal 58

A Bath Before Bed / Aleš Debeljak 60

American Home / Edward Nobles 61

The Bats This Summer / Stacie Cassarino 62

Oomph / Shawn R. Jones 63

New Year's Eve / Lisa Russ Spaar 64

About the Poets 65

Copyright Acknowledgments 75

Introduction

SINCE ITS FOUNDING IN 1975, Persea Books has been a vital force in contemporary poetry. In its early years, it was a publisher of indispensable poets in translation—Paul Celan, Nazim Hikmet, Osip Mandelstam, and Vasko Popa among them, as well as of innovative English-language poets like Paul Blackburn, Ramon Guthrie, Les Murray, and Laura Riding. Its participation at the inception of the National Poetry Series, publishing prizewinning books by Marie Howe, Thylias Moss, James Richardson, and others, further laid the groundwork for its ongoing contemporary American poetry program, which includes dynamic and varied poets like Cameron Awkward-Rich, Elizabeth Bradfield, Molly McCully Brown, Mitchell L. H. Douglas, Gabrielle Calvocoressi, Sarah Gambito, Kimberly Grey, Cynthia Marie Hoffman, Kimberly Johnson, Sandra Meek, Patrick Rosal, Lisa Russ Spaar, Alexandra Teague, and dozens of others—some of whom joined us by way of the Lexi Rudnitsky First Book Prize and the Lexi Rudnitsky Editor's Choice Award.

However and Wherever We Are takes its title from the poem "On Living" from the collection *Things I Didn't Know I Loved* by Nazim Hikmet—the very first book of poetry we published. (Our *Poems of Nazim Hikmet* and his *Human Landscapes from My Country* are still an active part of our list.) The anthology brings together a sampling of poets essential to the press's identity in poetry over the past half-century. Each poem collected here originally appeared in a monograph—a book of poems by the respective author—most of which remain in print to this day. Small yet formidable (like Persea itself), *However and Wherever We Are* is a showcase for many of the irreplaceable poets that Persea has published and continues to publish—poets of striking imagination, lyricism, insight, and conscience. We hope you enjoy these poems, and thank you, our readers, for your ongoing engagement and support of independent publishing. Here's to the next fifty years!

—Gabriel Fried, Poetry Editor

HOWEVER AND WHEREVER WE ARE

The Film

Come, let's go in.
The ticket-taker
has shyly grinned
and it's almost time,
Lovely One.
Let's go in.

The wind tonight's too wild.
The sky too deep,
too thin. Already it's time.
The lights have dimmed.
Come, Loveliest.
Let's go in

and know these bodies
we do not have to own, passing
quietly as dreams, as snow.
Already leaves are falling
and music begins.
Lovely One,

it's time.
Let's go in.

In Preparation

Explorer, what will you wear? Has someone taken
hair pulled from her brush each morning
since your birth, put it away in a box,
top carved with your name by your father
on the day he thought of your name?
Has she spun the long, fine stuff into thread
then knitted it into socks to warm you?
And the pony your sisters rode, that you,
a boy, harnessed and drove over broken
winter fields, each furrow imagined sastrugi—
has its skin been tanned, cured, and sewn
into mittens?
    More than your bunk
on the ship, more than the tent pitched on ice,
these will be home to you: layers that hold
your own warmth close, not letting it be lost to air
which itself is not prepared for what your arrival has begun.

from Ode to Anna Moffo

My debut is dark—
a kindergarten cameo
appearance playing imported tambourine.
    I stood on the stage
and rattled a white disk, waiting
for the curtain to drape my futility.
    Reward for ceaseless
    and timely
performance was candy corn.
I bit the black stripe off the triangle and saved the heart

of the confection—
an orange, blunt pyramid—for a day
when I could comprehend its antecedents.
    We learned to read notes
by a perverse pedagogy;
semibreves hovered outside the pale of clef
    or staff, and we guessed
    pitch by faith,
deprived of system. I gripped,
with the will of a colonialist, my tambourine,

    as if it were sky
    stirred, jangled,
and abandoned by a boy's hand,
as if the sky depended on a boy to make it sound.

On Living

I

Living is no laughing matter:
      you must live with great seriousness
           like a squirrel, for example—
  I mean without looking for something beyond and above living,
          I mean living must be your whole occupation.
Living is no laughing matter:
      you must take it seriously,
      so much so and to such a degree
  that, for example, your hands tied behind your back,
          your back to the wall,
  or else in a laboratory
      in your white coat and safety glasses,
      you can die for people—
  even for people whose faces you've never seen,
  even though you know living
      is the most real, the most beautiful thing.
I mean, you must take living so seriously
  that even at seventy, for example, you'll plant olive trees—
  and not for your children, either,
  but because although you fear death you don't believe it,
  because living, I mean, weighs heavier.

II

Let's say we're seriously ill, need surgery—
which is to say we might not get up
         from the white table.
Even though it's impossible not to feel sad
        about going a little too soon,
we'll still laugh at the jokes being told,

we'll look out the window to see if it's raining,
or still wait anxiously
                    for the latest newscast . . .
Let's say we're at the front—
            for something worth fighting for, say.
There, in the first offensive, on that very day,
        we might fall on our face, dead.
We'll know this with a curious anger,
        but we'll still worry ourselves to death
        about the outcome of the war, which could last years.
Let's say we're in prison
and close to fifty,
and we have eighteen more years, say,
                before the iron doors will open.
We'll still live with the outside,
with its people and animals, struggle and wind—
                I mean with the outside beyond the walls.
I mean, however and wherever we are,
        we must live as if we will never die.

III

This earth will grow cold,
a star among stars
            and one of the smallest,
a gilded mote on blue velvet—
            I mean *this*, our great earth.
This earth will grow cold one day,
not like a block of ice
or a dead cloud even
but like an empty walnut it will roll along

in pitch-black space . . .
You must grieve for this right now
—you have to feel this sorrow now—
for the world must be loved this much
              if you're going to say "I lived" . . .

translated from the Turkish by Randy Blasing and Mutlu Konuk

[Cut buds bloom awhile in a water glass]

Cut buds bloom awhile in a water glass
and demonstrate the perfect grace

that comes with dying. What am I saying?
I am saying that I love to be alive,

but love's a violent feeling. I'm powerless
beside the honey bees who have no cares

but industry. Kindness is important work
but I am weak. I'm not the woman

I thought I'd be. What kind of heaven
is available only to the dead?

If I were a clover in the lawn I'd have more sway
with myself, I'd tender more to gentleness.

In another life I walk a mile to the train
past a pair of red lions offering their fangs.

Invocation

River, what are you? Song of water too
pretty for the mouth, finger to scrawl.
Place we drink from, place we drown.
River above my head, daring to pour down
all the family secret, this invisible wet crown
where in the ear the words are *chunnel* and *resound*,
resound, and sound and sound, the dirty chamber
shutting the mouth, its levy, impound, its rain
hammering its round, a river above my head
making no sound, the secret in not ever out
bound, its bound, unbound. River, what are you?
River I drink from. River in which I drown.

Bioluminescence

Seconds passed. I watched one wave approach,
rolling through waters lit with jellyfish,
rolling obliquely landward till it crashed,
its ghostly aura scrawled across the beach.
And though I'd never seen a night that burned
with such intensity, it was your grace
that filled the room, your sleepy, owl-bright gaze
that followed as I closed the blinds. I turned,
& without thinking, pressed my face between
your breasts, where I could hear each lung draw air,
where I could hear the doors of your heart open
& shut methodically beneath my ear.
And nothing like this happened again. And yet
it happened then. It happened. I was there.

She Ties My Bowtie

What you thought was the sound of the deer drinking
at the base of the ravine was not their soft tongues
entering the water but my Love tying my bow tie.
We were in our little house just up from the ravine.
Forgive yourself. It's easy to mistake her wrists
for the necks of deer. Her fingers move so deftly.
One could call them skittish, though not really because
they aren't afraid of you. I know. You thought it was the deer
but they're so far down you couldn't possibly hear them.
No, this is the breeze my Love makes when she ties me up
and sends me out into the world. Her breath
pulled taut and held until she's through. I watch her
in the mirror, not even looking at me. She's so focused
on the knot and how to loop the silk into a bow.

[Take, for joy's sake, from these hands of mine]

Take, for joy's sake, from these hands of mine
A little honey and a little sunlight
As the bees of Persephone once ordered us to do.

We cannot cast adrift an unmoored boat,
Nor hear a shadow shoed in fur,
Nor conquer fear in this tangled dreaming life.

All we have left to us are kisses,
Sheathed in down like tiny bees
That die as they scatter from the hive.

They rustle in the translucent recesses of the night,
Their homeland is Taigetos' tangled woods,
Their food is honeysuckle, time, and mint.

So take, for joy's sake, this wild gift of mine,
This uninviting desiccated necklet
Made of dead bees that once turned honey into sunlight ·

translated from the Russian by Bernard Meares

Runaway Bride

Before they fell they waved like flags, the leaves,
and as they broke, there became a lovely order
to the dying.
                    The water spider moved
in no hurry at the bottom of the drained pond.

Everything seemed as it should.
                           Because I could
I even spent a while throwing apples

at a fence post. Over and over, my arm hurled
the poor things farther and farther

from the tree that had released them.

Two Drafts Written After a Fight

I.

Do I love you: yes or no?
The question: Is love a figure of speech?
I do—sometimes. Everyone wonders about our love; still,
there can be no doubt I have been true (almost always).
Happily remembering the start of our romance; it seemed
so promising . . .
And is love continual happiness or not?
Is not what matters?
I cannot tell you who I want to spend my life with.
Enough about our love.

II.

Do I love you? Yes or no—the question is, love,
a figure of speech. I do.
(Sometimes everyone wonders.)
About our love, still, there can be no doubt.
I have been true, almost always happily
remembering the start of our romance;
it seemed so promising, and is. Love,
continual happiness or not is not what matters.
I cannot tell you, who I want to spend my life with,
enough about our love.

A Difficult System

I love a man who is difficult to love, the way a horse is difficult to ride
when the horse is a man. Or when you don't stroke him enough, or you
do, but you stroke him wrongly and you don't love him completely.

I love the difficulty of loving a man incompletely. His blue, his black,
his back, I have not mounted enough, it's hard. The body is difficult,
even the horse's body, its muscled frame

always galloping away. Its mane, the main reason, I mean, is to stay,
to hold on, they're hard to know the difference between. I could say
that loving a man is an easy task. I could say the man and I are
beautiful like two horses

in the earliest, blurry light. Always love is useless. Or the horse is
because you don't know how to ride it and it can't run fast enough
or it runs too fast and there you are standing alone
in a field as it rushes

past you. Let's not mistake what's difficult here: the man, the manner
of loving him or leaving him. Or believing him, that his body wants
to be had easily by your body and not by any body
that can be simply had.

I love a man who is difficult to love, the way a man is difficult to love,
the way a horse that is running keeps on running so you will hold it
harder. So hold it harder, its continuously difficult body, then go on
loving him, easily, as hard.

Marriage

The real abbess of this convent just slipped into the parish photobooth
instead of preparing a proper liturgy. The liturgy was a
mess, inarticulate gibberish chanted by gardeners wearing rounds
of orange peel instead of spectacles, holding their books upside
down. I didn't even notice. I was sending the picture to you. You,
in pressed shirt, body of pink-edged sulphur, bedstraw hawkmoth,
white-lined sphinx, so elemental and beautiful, I'm filled
with anger and hunger, in other words love.

[As the weather warms]

As the weather warms year after year, aspens move higher up the draws, and the mesas are green into September. Eagles hunt over Red Canyon, hawks keep watch in the pines, and ospreys dip into the streams. It is late in the season when the waxwings gorge themselves on chokecherries, lift as one, spin above the hay fields, and head for the prairie.

Some History of Field Work

Then November seemed like a whole other gender:
the veins of wet leaves splayed upon the bedrock.
Skin of the land beneath which you could hear
your own blood rushing boyhood out. Under orders now
to be a man, I lie down on a large nurse tree, a fallen log
feeding the rest of the forest with its body; long scar
down birch bark. Please let this be enough. After awhile
I get hungry, too, my tongue a useless fruit. But I will lie
here until something sings be this. Birds, back me up—
you who leave your first feathers in the brambles.
For years, men had to hide their porn in the woods.
Desire in exile, insects running in rows. We boys
quickly gathering in the reedy ditch to see. Little hands—
we were hardly what the ladybugs were looking for.
But we held the centerfold sideways until it was taken
by the wind. Only by waiting did we come to wanting.
Now, there are switches in the air; I can't stay here.
The trout grow so cold they leap into the trees, become
the stars above this boreal forest. Still, I
would like to be a man, to see what that might lead to.

Tornados

Truth is, I envy them
not because they dance; I out jitterbug them
as I'm shuttled through and through legs
strong as looms, weaving time. They
do black more justice than I, frenzy
of conductor of philharmonic and electricity, hair
on end, result of the charge when horns and strings release
the pent up Beethoven and Mozart. Ions played

instead of notes. The movement
is not wrath, not hormone swarm because
I saw my first forming above the church a surrogate
steeple. The morning of my first baptism and
salvation already tangible, funnel for the spirit
coming into me without losing a drop, my black
guardian angel come to rescue me before all the words

get out, I looked over Jordan and what did I see coming for
to carry me home. Regardez, it all comes back, even the first
grade French, when the tornado stirs up the past, bewitched spoon
lost in its own spin, like a roulette wheel that won't
be steered, like the world. They drove me underground,
tornado watches and warnings, atomic bomb drills. Adult
storms so I had to leave the room. Truth is

the tornado is a perfect nappy curl, tightly wound,
spinning wildly when I try to tamper with its nature, shunning
the hot comb and pressing oil even though if absolutely straight
I'd have the longest hair in the world. Bouffant tornadic
crown taking the royal path on a trip to town, stroll down
Tornado Alley where it intersects Memory Lane. Smoky spirit-
clouds, shadows searching for what cast them.

PAUL BLACKBURN

Ritual X.: The Evening Pair of Ales

EAST OF EDEN
is mountains & desert
until you cross the passes into India .
It is 3 o'clock in the afternoon or
twenty of 8 at night, depending
            which clock you believe .

AND WEST IS WEST
It's where the cups and saucers are,
the plates, the knives and forks .

            The turkey sandwich comes alone
            or with onions if you like
The old newspaperman always takes his hat off
& lays it atop the cigarette machine;
the younger, so-hip journalist, leaves his on
old-style .

The old man sits down in the corner, puts
            his hat back on. No challenge, but
                it's visible, the beau geste .
                    The cigarette
hangs from the side of the younger man's mouth, he's
putting himself on .
            East of Eden is mountains & desert & every
                thing creeps up on you & comes in the night,
                    unexpectedly.
when one would least put out his hand
to offer, or to defend .

21

Museum of Science and History

Growing up black white trash you grow up
the only and complete / Whale skeleton
In the local mammals wing

Of a museum of science and history in a land-locked state
You grow up Lord   bigger and smaller than you are and were
You grow up white

But not a white that counts it makes
People uncomfortable
who when they think of white think of linoleum

You grow up a display case   Lord in which
Two hares have been arranged to illustrate
The influence of environment on coloring

The one   / Brown as the dirt it dies in
the other so white it disappears behind the glare

N'Jadaka's Appeal

Hey Auntie! Can you spare me
a homeland? The one I left
didn't gift me my mother's
name. Every word I'm fighting
for: my native tongue, my immortal.

Hey Auntie. Let us carve me a tongue
to lick these wounds scriptured
on my skin. They sting, they linger,
they read as abscess—or absence;
I never learned the difference.

Hey, Auntie, maybe you could
fix your face to love me. I know
I spit chaos, but if you cut out
my tongue I will write you
a psalm, a shadow, a love song.

Hey Auntie? Why do men metaphor
mothers into countries, into tongues?
I wouldn't know. I've never had
a country. I mean, a mother.
I mean, a home. I mean, a tongue.

Today Is Friday

Always it was going on
In the white hollow roar
you could hear it at a hundred paces if you listened closely
and a hemisphere away if you didn't listen at all
if you were paying no attention to it
fixing your mind hard on something else
   I will not hear it
   I will not hear it
   I

Screaming it inwardly so hard it seemed
your seminal vesicles must rupture with the strain
you could hear it close at hand
feel it crimping your nerve ends
your brain pack buckling in its grip

see it perform its curious rituals
as pale as ichor
limp as larvae
You could curl up with it and sleep
   Only it was not
   Only it was not
   Only it

You could taste it being fed intravenously though a
skein of tubes into your most plausible dreams
It was happening It was going on as suavely
as if it were a rank of drop-forges
smashing diamonds to dust as fast as
they could be fed to them.

Tangible
It is a great protracted
totally transparent cube
with sides and angles
perceptibly contracting against
eyeballs and nose and mouth and skin

It is always happening
It is always going on
When it gets tired of going on
maybe it will stop

Part of Eve's Discussion

It was like the moment when a bird decides not to eat from your hand,
and flies, just before it flies, the moment the rivers seem to still
and stop because a storm is coming, but there is no storm, as when
a hundred starlings lift and bank together before they wheel and drop,
very much like the moment, driving on bad ice, when it occurs to you
your car could spin, just before it slowly begins to spin, like
the moment just before you forgot what it was you were about to say,
it was like that, and after that, it was still like that, only
all the time.

O

mountainous
appetite!
how flat
we'd find
the view
without you!

Raw Bar

Why does it feel so good? you murmured while
losing consciousness after wave on wave
smashed into you & shook you to the bone.

Before going under, you had been kind
enough to steer me in the right direction
(up). I took it to the next level: congress

with you, the two of us joined at the hip,
less like a bicameral legislature
than a bivalve—one of the Raspberry Point,

Poppasquash, or Lady Chatterley oysters
that we'd washed down, each of them held together
by just a hinge of skin the same as us.

You were the shore, I was the wave that broke
against you after building in the ocean.

Ode on My Episiotomy

Forget pearls, lace-edged kerchiefs, roomy pleats—
this is my most matronly adornment:
stitches purling up the middle of me
to shut my seam, the one that jagged gaped
upon my fecund, unspeakable dark,
my indecorum needled together
with torquemadan efficiency.
But O! the dream of the dropped stitch! the loophole
through which that unruly within might thread,
catch with a small snag, pull the fray, unknit
the knots unnoticed, and undoily me.

Don't lock up the parlor yet; such pleasure
in unraveling, I may take up the sharps
and darn myself to ladylike again.

Nonsomnolent

We wake ardent, we wake
concave, open our eyes
in a snit of singularity.

We wake wily
at the business end
of ongoing diminishment.

We wake after dreams
so arch, so full of twee
villainy, it's no wonder

we're always getting up
to leave. Nightgowns
are errant around legs

and torsos, so we wake
without them. We wake
sweat saronged, latticeless.

We wake to a breast
garden—pretty much
what everyone has always

suspected. Our sleep
pends, diasporic. We sleep
unctuously in summer.

Our love is official
now. We are an institution
unto each other. When

she ships her legs
to the mattress's farthest
admonition, it is breath

breaking. We wake
in brazen arrangements.
You wonder

so I'll tell you: we are
incredible in bed.

Meditations in an Emergency

I wake up & it breaks my heart. I draw the blinds & the thrill of
rain breaks my heart. I go outside. I ride the train, walk among the
buildings, men in Monday suits. The flight of doves, the city of tents
beneath the underpass, the huddled mass, old women hawking roses,
& children all of them, break my heart. There's a dream I have in
which I love the world. I run from end to end like fingers through her
hair. There are no borders, only wind. Like you, I was born. Like you,
I was raised in the institution of dreaming. Hand on my heart. Hand
on my stupid heart.

from A Language of Hemophilia

hemo
philia

'blood'
'affection for'

trans
fusion

hema
toma

patho
genesis

anti
body

hyper
trophy

bio
assay

cry
cryo

precipitate
precipice

What I Would Ask You

Friend,
when the end comes,
who takes the blood from us?

The earth or the air—

Which did you choose—

Assisi

Umbrian night.
Umbrian night with the silver of churchbell and olive leaf.
Umbrian night with the stone that you carried here.
Umbrian night with the stone.

> Dumb, that which rose into life, dumb.
> Refill the jugs, come.

Earthenware jug.
Earthenware jug to which the potter's hand grew affixed.
Earthenware jug which a shade's hand closed for ever.
Earthenware jug with a shade's seal.

> Stone, wherever you look, stone.
> Let the grey animal in.

Trotting animal.
Trotting animal in the snow the nakedest hand scatters.
Trotting animal before the word that clicked shut.
Trotting animal that takes sleep from the feeding hand.

> Brightness that will not comfort, brightness you shed.
> Still they are begging, Francis—the dead.

translated from the German by Michael Hamburger

Continuum

After days of murder, more bodies
than nights in a week, you would think
we'd say Enough. Instead,
more blood. Don't think
it's just the dealers, that side
of law not in your nature.
It's expectant fathers on morning walks,
it's businessmen minding their business,
selling denim on Sunday afternoons.
Yesterday, my student who doesn't believe
in gun control, said he wanted to write
a poem about parenting & the right
to bear arms, how slipping on one side
affects the other
(you guess
            which way that goes).
& though you won't find me w/steel
in the small of my back (@ least
not by my hand), I know the peace
a poem can bring. So I say, Yes,
write. & he goes back to his seat
nodding his head, the room filled
w/the voices of his classmates
comparing Dove, Simic, & Wright,
the push of my chair
back from my desk to stand & speak
like fingernails
on a chalk board, like a scream
when a gun fires.

The Central Virginia Training Center

formerly The Virginia State Colony for Epileptics and Feebleminded

Whatever it is—
home or hospital,
graveyard or asylum,
government facility or great
tract of land slowly ceding
itself back to dust—

its church is a low-slung brick box
with a single window,
a white piece of plywood
labeled chapel, and a locked door.

Whatever it is,
my mother and I ride along
its red roads in February
with the windows down:
this place looks lived in,
that one has stiff, gray curtains
in the window, a roof caving in.

We see a small group moving
in the channel between one building
and the next, bowing in an absent wind.

He is in a wheelchair, she is stumbling,
pushing a pram from decades ago,
coal black and wrong. There is no way
it holds a baby. Behind them,
a few more shuffling bodies in coats.

I am my own kind of damaged there,
looking out the right-hand window.
Spastic, palsied and off-balance,
I'm taking crooked notes about this place.

It is the land where he is buried, the place
she spent her whole life, the room
where they made it impossible
for her to have children.

It is the colony where he did not learn to read,
but did paint every single slat of fence
you see that shade of yellow.

The place she didn't want to leave
when she finally could,
because she'd lived there fifty years,
and couldn't drive a car, or remember
the outside, or trust anyone
to touch her gently.

And, by some accident of luck or grace,
some window less than half a century wide,
it is my backyard but not what happened
to my body—

Torsion

Each tendon's tender ribbon
pushed against the machine,
against metal pins mapping
the length of my leg—you work
my furious body, work my body
mean and loose—my body
humming metal—each pin a flag
in numbered, quartered land—
each pin a catch, a hitch that slows
the tendons' stretch—and each tendon
tightens, stops short, a horse
restive in its blinders resisting
the rider's urge and spur—your hands
the hands that hold the course,
that gentle and tender, loosen
and numb, drive headlong—
my body blind and dumb,
bridled or yoked, broken then
opened, run down into darkness,
run down—your hands
the hands that carry me—
and the machine's teeth
sink down, and the machine
hauls its gears—into my body's
wild and all its dangers—

What Silence Equals

Where the homogenous wind beats the wild grass closer to the quiet
   ground
Homogenous, wild, quiet,
Homogeny in a pretense of superiority
Beats wildness to wither into nothingness,
The quiet ground enveloping all that is askew, unorthodox,
The chaff of the world.
If we keep our heads bent in equal direction
Like plow horses pulling against the elements,
The plow will conform into manageability the unharrowed.

The plow will conform into manageability the unharrowed.
Plow, conform, unharrowed
Like strong men at the circus with handlebar mustaches
We hold up this principle while the applause meter goes berserk.
We watch mute and emotionless as you pace in your cage,
Your frenzied wildness eating you up alive,
Giving back to the god-given earth what you took.
If we're not better than you, what are we better than?
Let the saber-toothed plow of silence reign.

Let the saber-toothed plow of silence reign.
Saber-toothed, silence, reign
We watch you rise fitfully with fever in your apartment,
Your eyelids bruised from crying.
Mute and emotionless we watch you make phone calls
And talk a steady stream of what you need and believe.
Your so-called friends sit paralyzed on the other end;
They've said they love you,
But what good can be done really for a drowning man?
In time your talk will collapse onto itself like a Chinese box.
They'll admire the inlay of pain on your face.

They just want to commute conscience-free to their jobs.
Like a Chinese box you'll be buried with all your secret drawers locked.

Like a Chinese box you'll be buried with all your secret drawers locked.
Box, buried, secret
Ugly angels like buzzards circle overhead.
Your prayers, their prey, they carry clenched between their teeth.
On the horizon we stand, appointed klansmen waiting,
Impatient for the riffraff around us to cancel itself out.
Our tuft heads in the distance project a cryptic kind of village—
We're just a discriminating denomination, folks.
You sink, rightly so, in the swamp of your made bed,
Far enough away so you can't infect the kids in our schools.
The sky cuts you off like a sun roof as it should.

The sky cuts you off like a sun roof as it should.
Cuts, off, should
Your screams billow up, clouding the glass.
We watch your face, contorted, shrink and whirl away
With a high-pitched cry like a helium balloon losing its air.
We watch several faces follow yours
As if severed from some grasp,
Each with that high-pitched ringing noise.
They shrink and whirl away behind the cloudy glass of the sky.
We watch until that irritating ring stops in our ears,
Comforted by the solid surface of the god-given earth
Where the homogeneous wind beats the wild grass closer to the quiet
    ground.

Ode to Flint, Michigan, Five Years, Three Months, Ten Days after the Water Crisis Began

In the city where I was born,
my daughter cannot

use the water:
to rinse her curls

could stop her growing,
slam the storm doors shut.

Where I've dreamed
her tall,

eclipsed by daylight,
this city follows,

every shadow
unmoving.

I take my things
to the map edge,

& the city comes home
shouting.

Police on the lawn.
City with coals for hands.

City, city
every
where

& not a drop
to drink.

Milwaukee, 1968

Say it loud! I'm Black and I'm Proud—James Brown

I was there the day black stopped
being the worst thing you could call somebody.
Right on 16th Street between Friebrantz
and Olive. The day before, the exact same word
could get you beat up or spanked, but that morning
we turned on the radio and it was as if the sun had come out
of the closet, as if the moon was burning her underwear.
And we didn't just stand around and watch
either. Me, Michael, Sherrie, David,
and Theresa—we marched up and down the street
singing ourselves into brand new people,
doing our part to free the nation.
And when the street lights came on, I marched
right up the stairs to our second floor flat
still singing loud and proud, praying my mother
had heard we weren't colored anymore, kind of worried
and yet no turning back, marching around
the kitchen table, was not going to be moved,
finally peeking over at my mother washing dishes,
spying her trying not to laugh
and wonder who I'd be if she'd done the opposite,
if by the following week we weren't both wearing afros.

Rain at Reading

We had gathered under a tent in the park
for some words before lunch and after separate mornings,
and when—twice—the poet said "capital,"
the lightning bolts that followed the noun
had me bolting too; I'd always suspected
God's communist leanings, but now I regretted
how few exchanges we know
between craft and climate:

imagine a rhyme inciting a rainbow,
blood feuds bruising the sky,
hymns of forgiveness bringing a soft
new light to the faces watching the last act,
waltzes and songs and declamations—
this would be capital entertainment!—
locked in a clinch with open air.

But the lightning was as quick as it was loud.
The clouds dispersed,
and then so did the crowd.

Song

I found my muster station, sir.
My skin is patent leather.
The tourists are recidivists.
This calm is earthquake weather.

I've used up all the mulligans.
I'd kill to share a vice.
The youngster reads a yellowed Oui.
The socialite has lice.

The Europe trip I finally took
was rash and Polaroid,
was gilt, confit, and bathhouse foam.
And I cannot avoid

the end: I will not die in Paris,
won't rest for good behind
a painted mausoleum door.
The purser will not find

me mummified beneath your tulle,
and Paris will not burn.
Today is Thursday, so I'll die.
Come help me pick my urn.

Jocks

The back row in American History,
already wearing away uniforms
under our warm-ups, popping purple gum,
some of us in lipstick stolen from our mothers,
others mistaken for our younger brothers,
with buzz cuts, cornrows, jacked-up ponytails,
we didn't care about the presidents.
We cut out early in a seamless blitz
of nylon sheen. Our thighs were staggering,
our stretches legendary: counting *four,*
five, sex, we swore we saw the bleachers flinch.
We licked our palms and rubbed our sneakers clean
and couldn't stand the Pentecostal teams
with their set shots and culottes—what was worse
than modesty? And who could top our coach,
destroying clipboards, screaming, GET YOUR MAN!,
whose fury was the only compliment
we'd ever trusted? Most of us believed
that suffrage meant *collective suffering.*
We weren't discerning but we weren't unsure.
Our trick plays worked. We wore each other's sweat.
Our pregnant captain didn't know it yet.

Team

There's no I in team,
but there's one in bitterness
and one in failure.

I Am Not from the Philippines

A white guy liked me and it was like
a lake might bend in half.

I wanted to go to The Olive Garden.
I said Yes with my eyes like platelets.

When God was Filipino,
he put a pig and fire together and called it porkissimo.

I grabbed a Filipino girl's hand and she said are you a lesbian.
I faked it to myself. I faked it to them all.

All the nurses ever, ever in the world
are Filipino.

Like a push in the gut, I rush past the hovels of hospital rooms.
The great digital of machines and humans simmering at work.

The pork chop of the leg poking from the blanket.
There will always be sick people. You'll always have a job.

Nurses with their white soft shoes. Their cuneiform writing.
The change purses of nurses divoting around.

My aunts mothers uncles cousins whiplashing into nurses.

3 October

Dear Editor:

Please consider the enclosed poems for publication. They are from my manuscript, *X = Pawn Capture*, a lyrical study of a particular kind of chess game played within my family: the first move has to be made by someone who doesn't understand the basic rules. My grandmother didn't like this game, and usually, when the wind, drifting as it did by the kitchen as she baked, brought something in as if a gift, something like berry scent or that of the sweet mixed grasses, she would lean out with a smile as if remembering a saint, one she knew personally, one she took personally. *Which saint?* I'd ask, and she would make it up: *Saint Berry*, she'd say, picking up a rook and swishing it around the board. *Saint Berry, who protested the loss of her virginity by heaping ash and kindling on the dinner of her betrayer.* She'd move the piece in the air and place it somewhere on a white square. *All right old man, you got your way.* And later there'd be cabbages in red sauce and a half glass of wine.

Thank you for your consideration, and for reading. I have enclosed an SASE, and look forward to hearing from you.

Sincerely,
Amy Newman

Road Scatter

A single vibration breaks the story
to the crystal remnants
of perfect pitch. A wheelflung
pebble, and sun
pierces the windshield's tint.
The next days
spider the glass. The heart
is damage, a small pit: for wheelflung
pebble, substitute
bullet, and the tire, still
rotating mid-air, catches
the last rayed light: the camera's
pinhole a magnet
for angels, a needle's eye clustered
with crushed wings. Flight
didn't survive the breakage.
What we filmed was landing.

The Stork

When the stork fishes us out
from the marshes, we are just
opening our eyes to the cloud
of its body wobbling above us
half of it white half of it
black storm, its beak of black
rain stabbing into the waters.
What else could we remember?
The sound of its wings like
umbrellas snapping open
on the wind, the view
from our sling, the air
sliced open and wisping
past the belly of the bird,
whirling on the other side of flight.
The city comes like a barge
lumbering through the grasses.
Chimneys widen and sway
beneath us. The stork
knows the address, the fireplace
at which our mothers
stoop, her arms outstretched.
Her pale hands
signal like a water lily
blooming in the depths.
When the beak
opens, the darkness takes
us, wipes our minds
with soot so there is
only the long fall, the

touch of human skin. Our
boundedness to earth. What
we remember.

You Can Always Freeze Your Eggs

I can't face my body when the evening
is over and one by one everyone grows
with their families toward evening and evening
and alone to my apartment I go

It's me and the buzz of the fridge, the fridge
is me, my opera, my anthem, my buzz, my ballad
My body, she drifts over the bridge
while I worry about the planted

irises gone rotten, were they a prophecy?
I worry my fuzzy eggs are stacked
in my ovaries' hapless pockets
like the cartons of mush I scrapped

since I forgot all March and April
as they squatted in the dark fridge
Today I break each month in the pail
one at a time, smashing each shell on the ridge

smashing them because I didn't know
smashing the months because I forgot, because I can't
forget, smashing because I didn't hear the bells or feel the toll
and I have to break them to see them run

Black Line

Angles-sur-Anglin, France

Where families slept and built
their fires against the limestone wall
animals move out of rock: lion, horse, ibex,
and in the center three women, sculpted,
one belly marked with the dark
line of pregnancy,
the birthing out through
muscle and stone, fur
to fur, dark
pigment of the belly and hairy
thatch—yes, I see now,
I see us tunneling through, time
and again. Animals
on their haunches or
looking over their shoulders.
Oh, if only we saw them
painted in the dark, etched
or sculpted, if only we stopped
to look and rubbed our fingers
along their bodies. Long the birthing, bones
forced open, the tunnel taking us,
our gyrations against
wet walls, life
pushed out, sent on, sent on.
We don't know
if we are alive—stone,
air, flesh—what borders
did we cross?

Xī'ān Nocturne with Jasmine and Pears

I call my mother to tell her about a rare dream
in the first language:

> the fruit vendor's miniature green pears
> the soft juice I crave

> she pays but gets the wrong change
> & I realize she can't read the words
> on the cardboard sign and doesn't know
> how much she is owed

she reminds me that the word for pear
sounds the same as the word for leave
   梨 (lí) and 离 (lí)
you're telling me I paid too great a price
to leave, she says

inflected differently, 莉 (lì) is jasmine
   my mother's namesake

how do I tell her that a week earlier, leaving
my grandparents' home, an ambush of jasmine
stopped me on the sidewalk—small mouths
muted with grime yet still sweet as a raindipped
stone

    I plucked one
tucked its velvet trumpet behind my ear

now half a world away
   my mouth empties:
every word sounds the same

Anyway

The way an acre of starlings towers and pours
rapidly through itself, a slipping knot,
landing so few feet down the furrows (the whole skywriting
like a secret no one knows they have given away)
is one of those breathtaking wastes
(sun and the seeds they feed on being others)
in which something senseless, even selfish, absurdly magnified,
becomes grandeur (love is another).
Sometime the flock, banking in unison,
vanishes an instant, like a sheet of paper edge-on
(a secret, anyway, is the illusion
confession it would make a difference).
I watched this happen once—two seconds, hours—
till I understood no kindness, not a shadow or stone.
And they did not come back,
though I waited all evening (and it was you
I waited for). Though the sky turned black.

Children Walk on Chairs to Cross a Flooded Schoolyard

Taytay, Rizal Province, Philippines (based on the photo by Noel Celis)

Hardly anything holds the children up, each poised
mid-air, barely the ball of one small foot
kissing the chair's wood, so
they don't just step across, but pause
above the water. I look at that cotton mangle
of a sky, post-typhoon, and presume
it's holding something back. In this country,
it's the season of greedy gods
and the several hundred cathedrals
worth of water they spill onto little tropic villages
like this one, where a girl is likely to know
the name of the man who built
every chair in her school by hand,
six of which are now arranged
into a makeshift bridge so that she and her mates
can cross their flooded schoolyard.
Boys in royal blue shorts and red rain boots,
the girls brown and bare-toed
in starch white shirts and pleated skirts.
They hover like bells that can choose
to withhold their one clear, true
bronze note, until all this nonsense
of wind and drizzle dies down.
One boy even reaches forward
into the dark sudden pool below
toward someone we can't see, and
at the same time, without looking, seems
to offer the tips of his fingers back to the smaller girl
behind him. I want the children
ferried quickly across so they can get back

to slapping one another on the neck
and cheating each other at checkers.
I've said time and time again I don't believe
in mystery, and then I'm reminded what it's like
to be in America, to kneel beside
a six-year-old, to slide my left hand
beneath his back and my right under his knees,
and then carry him up a long flight of stairs
to his bed. I can feel the fine bones,
the little ridges of the spine
with my palm, the tiny smooth stone
of the elbow. I remember I've lifted
a sleeping body so slight I thought
the whole catastrophic world could fall away.
I forget how disaster works, how it can turn
a child back into glistening butterfish
or finches. And then they'll just do
what they do, which is teach the rest of us
how to move with such natural gravity.
Look at these two girls, center frame,
who hold out their arms
as if they're finally remembering
they were made for other altitudes.
I love them for the peculiar joy
of returning to earth. Not an ounce
of impatience. This simple thrill
of touching ground.

A Bath Before Bed

If I pull back, because I can't stand
how pain can only recognize more pain,
it will come after me, dark and shivering
with a power I feel even now: this rhythm
one part peace and one desire,
tempo made in the image of prayer
will be looking for me,
will find me in a town without a name,
where beggars and sinners
who want to be kids again
are chased away, the watchman
shooing me from the fountain.
My throat is dry, I understand
even less than before.
Less and less certain that a piece
of the past is alive, even now,
in some cellar below the mind,
insisting like an oath to the secret
that makes me rinse your back,
up and down, a familiar stroke,
a damp cloth over your hips,
the soapy water rising to steam
and softening me like clay
that works and in its joyful task
is done. Today, at least,
a tiny grace is mine.

American Home

Chippendale, American,
with curved aborted leaf
and reeded spool, circa 1802,
this bridal bed, though pine,
retains its mahogany
reddish hue, a result
of thickened ox blood
and fresh New England cream.
The high heels, hushed
from their seductive click,
look innocent, unable to lure
with motion or the meaningful
turn.
  I watched them fall,
each one alone, with seeming
intent, over the edge
of this tall
and vacant bed.

The Bats This Summer

Every sundown we start out
as clear forms. I am the daughter
walking beside the mother and
I am the mother pulling the daughter
through the darkening world and
I am no one's wife.
By the time we return
home we've become ourselves
mere vanishings. This is how night
is made. A few stars if we're lucky,
and the bats that swoop so near
as if they detect my fear—
how foolish I must look, cowering
for no reason while they wrest
any living matter whole.
My daughter gazes up
for each luminous thing my mother
is willing to affirm. Later, no one
will hold my worries. Like everything
else in summer, we move in circles,
chased by the longing for more.
More birdsong. More mountain. More moon.
I am trying to love even the ugly things
of this world. I am sure
they're coming for me.

Oomph

twists of lust, oiled gifts
to some graffiti, others rebellion,
but locks are the turf
where I land face first in soil
the strands, blades
the scalp, earth
the mane, hallucination,
each lock a spirit spinning
kaleidoscopic limb
twined around my waist.
I can't unravel myself
this time. He kisses
down sepia brown spine.
Knows where to turn. Skin
forsakes me again.
I might have to
go through this flame. Tonight,
I have this tickle,
this itch—intense hunger,
death of light.

LISA RUSS SPAAR

New Year's Eve

I'm a sucker for a gothic ending:
for example, this opal brooch of sky,
like milk tinged with blood

behind a leaden fret of branches,
the year going down, distant as nursery glow,
natal and passionate.

Returning to my car at dusk
along an alley of tall boxwoods
hiding private yards

—far-off houses, each extinguished
by a certain compromise and sadness,
my tongue stung with champagne

from a party I've just fled,
coat heavy on my shoulders,
reminder that all ways are one, at the last—

my throat stops suddenly with longing.
Not for what I still don't know,
but for what I have known, with you inside me:

blue on blue, and that fierce, white star.
Dark arteries. Splendor of hope's risk,
        still running there.

About the Poets

TOM ANDREWS (1961–2001) was awarded a Guggenheim Fellowship, the Rome Prize in Literature, and the Iowa Poetry Prize for *The Hemophiliac's Motorcycle*. He was a National Poetry Series Award winner for *The Brother's Country*, which Persea published in 1990.

JUBI ARRIOLA-HEADLEY is the author of the poetry collections *original kink* (recipient of the 2021 Housatonic Book Award) and *Bound*, which the Poetry Foundation described as "joyful and liberatory." His work has received support from Yaddo, Millay Arts, Lambda Literary, the Virginia Center for the Creative Arts, and the Atlantic Center for the Arts.

CAMERON AWKWARD-RICH is the author of three collections of poetry, *Sympathetic Little Monster*, *Dispatch* (a work of "beguiling lyric," according to *The New Yorker*), and *An Optimism*, as well as an important work of trans theory, *The Terrible We: Thinking with Trans Maladjustment*. His creative work has been supported by fellowships from Cave Canem, The Watering Hole, and the Lannan Foundation.

AARON BELZ, dubbed "the comic poet of the apocalypse" by Rae Armantrout, is the author of *The Bird Hoverer*; *Lovely, Raspberry*; *Glitter Bomb*; and *Soft Launch*.

PAUL BLACKBURN (1926–1971) was a Black Mountain Poet, editor, literary organizer, and a translator of Provençal troubadour verse—a friend, collaborator, and supporter of many poets in the Beat and Deep Image, and New York School poetry movements.

RANDY BLASING is the author of numerous books of poetry, most recently *A Change of Heart* and *Sweet Crude*, and the acclaimed co-translator from the Turkish of Persea's editions of the poetry of Nazim Hikmet. He has received grants from the Ingram Merrill Foundation and a translation fellowship from the National Endowment for the Arts.

ELIZABETH BRADFIELD is a writer, educator, and naturalist. Among her many admired books are the poetry collections *SOFAR, Toward Antarctica, Once Removed, Approaching Ice,* and *Interpretive Work.* She is founder and editor-in-chief of *Broadsided,* and she spends much of her life at sea.

MOLLY MCCULLY BROWN's books, *The Virginia State Colony for Epileptics and Feebleminded,* a New York Times Editors Choice, and *Places I've Taken My Body: Essays,* have established her as one of the most important voices on disability writing today. And she is also the co-author, with Susannah Nevison, of *In the Field Between Us,* an epistolary poetry collection about disability and friendship. Among her awards and honors are the Amy Lowell Poetry Traveling Scholarship and a United States Artists Fellowship.

GABRIELLE CALVOCORESSI is the author of three daring, redemptive, and paradigm-shifting collections of poetry: *The Last Time I Saw Amelia Earhart; Apocalyptic Swing,* a finalist for the LA Times Book Prize; and *Rocket Fantastic,* winner of the Publishing Triangle's Audre Lorde Award.

SARAH CARSON is the author of three collections, including *How to Baptize a Child in Flint, Michigan,* an eye-opening collection that brings the reader into the generational experiences of living, working, and loving in one of America's most forsaken communities. She has received grants and prizes from *Tin House,* the Illinois Arts Council, and Martha's Vineyard Institute of Creative Writing.

STACIE CASSARINO is the author of *Each Luminous Thing* (recommended by the *New York Times Book Review* and *Washington Post* Book Club); *Zero at the Bone,* which received a Lambda Literary Award and the Publishing Triangle's Audre Lorde Award; and *Culinary Poetics and Edible Images in Twentieth-Century American Literature,* a scholarly monograph.

PAUL CELAN (1920–1970) is the essential poet of the Holocaust, one of the greatest poets to ever write in German—and among the indispensable writers of the twentieth century in any language. His poems "embody a conviction that the truth of what has been broken and torn must be told with a jagged grace" (Robert Pinsky, *The New Republic*). For decades, Michael Hamburger's admired translations, published by Persea, have provided countless readers with access to Celan's poetry.

LAURA CRONK is the author of two ethereal poetry collections, *Having Been an Accomplice* and *Ghost Hour*. For many years, she curated the famous Monday Night Poetry Series at KGB Bar in New York City's East Village.

ALEŠ DEBELJAK (1961–2016) was an essential Slovenian translator, essayist, poet, and cultural critic. He was Director of the Center for Cultural and Religious Studies at the University of Ljubljana in Slovenia. Among his honors are the Slovenian National Book Award and the Poetry for Peace Prize from the Miriam Felicia Lindberg Memorial Peace Foundation.

TORY DENT (1958–2005) was a poet, essayist and art critic. She was the author of three books of poetry: *What Silence Equals*; *H.I.V.*, *Mon Amour*; and *Black Milk*, which portrayed her life and eventual illness following her diagnosis of H.I.V. in 1988—a diagnosis that transformed her, as a writer, into "a prophet of extremity, crying in the wilderness of a new world" (*Women's Review of Books*).

MITCHELL L. H. DOUGLAS is "a poet of both place and race who . . . sings of America in all its vice and virtue" (*Publishers Weekly*). His three books are *dying in the scarecrow's arms*, */blak/ /al-fə bet/*, and *Cooling Board: A Long Playing Poem*.

RACHEL GALVIN is the author of three exceptional collections of poetry, including *Uterotopia*. She is also a scholar, author of a scholarly monograph, *News of War: Civilian Poetry 1936–1945*, and an acclaimed translator from the French and Spanish, the recipient of a translation fellowship from the National Endowment for the Arts, and a finalist for the 2019 National Translation Award.

SARAH GAMBITO is the author of three collections of poetry, most recently *Loves You*, a book which "challenges readers to consider what sustains and nurtures them" (*Washington Post*). Her honors include the Barnes & Noble Writers for Writers Award from *Poets & Writers*, the Wai Look Award for Outstanding Service to the Arts from the Asian American Arts Alliance, and grants and fellowships from the National Endowment for the Arts and the New York Foundation for the Arts.

KIMBERLY GREY is the author of three innovative books: two collections of poetry, *Systems for the Future of Feeling* and *The Opposite of Light*, and *A Mother Is an Intellectual Thing*, a heartbreaking collection of essays on maternal rejection.

RAMON GUTHRIE (1896–1973) was a professor of French at Dartmouth College. He published five books of poetry, culminating in his masterpiece *Maximum Security Ward*, written when he was seventy years old and dying of cancer, and for which he won the Marjorie Peabody Waite Award of the National Academy of Arts and Letters. Although Guthrie was not well-known nor a member of any particular school of writing, he was regarded by critics of his day as one of the great American poets of the twentieth century.

NÂZIM HIKMET (1902–1963) is Turkey's best-loved poet, still a commanding presence in its public life. He was born into the elite of the Ottoman Empire, but embraced Communist ideals and joined the revolutionary ranks when he was nineteen. He was uncompromising in his politics, for which he spent more than twenty years in prisons or in exile. His stirring, unadorned verse was banned in Turkey from 1938 to 1965, yet his poems were passed from hand to hand and became immensely popular. Today, Hikmet's work is available in more than fifty languages, and he is recognized worldwide as a major twentieth-century poet. The English-language translations by Randy Blasing and Mutlu Konuk have been among Persea's signature publications.

CYNTHIA MARIE HOFFMAN is the author of the OCD memoir-in-prose-poems, *Exploding Head*, as well as three previous ingenious collections of poetry: *Sightseer, Paper Doll Fetus*, and *Call Me When You Want to Talk about the Tombstones*.

MARIE HOWE's first collection, *The Good Thief*, was selected by Margaret Atwood as part of the National Poetry Series and published by Persea in 1988. The book helped launch her as one of America's best and most beloved contemporary poets.

KIMBERLY JOHNSON is a distinguished poet, translator, and literary critic. She is the author of four incomparable books of poetry, all published by Persea, most recently *Fatal*. She is the recipient of grants and fellowships from the John Simon Guggenheim Foundation, the National Endowment for the Arts, the Utah Arts Council, and the Mellon Foundation.

SHAWN R. JONES is the author of *Date of Birth*, a moving collection set mostly in the Atlantic City of her youth. She is a member of the poetry performance troupe No River Twice.

WAYNE KOESTENBAUM is an acclaimed poet, novelist, artist, and cultural critic. He is the author of nineteen books, including three collections of poetry from Persea: *The Milk of Inquiry, Ode to Anna Moffo and Other Poems*, and *Rhapsodies of a Repeat Offender*.

ANNI LIU is the author of *Border Vista*, named a Best Poetry Book of 2022 by the *New York Times Book Review*, which called it "inviting, dark and quiet like a museum at night."

ANNE MARIE MACARI is the author of five inimitable collections of poetry, among them *Red Deer* and *Heaven Beneath*, which Ross Gay described as "a book that has its hands reaching out to you, and its soul reaching into the earth."

OSIP MANDELSTAM (1891–1938) was one of the most significant

Russian poets of the twentieth century, and his work has achieved global status. Associated with the school of Acmeism, Mandelstam grounded his lyric writing in the concrete and the historic, illuminating how pasts shine through present human experience, as well as how human fragility and what he termed the "noise of time" imprint civilizations. A prophet of human dignity and freedom, Mandelstam died in a transit camp in 1938 at the height of Stalin's purges.

RANDALL MANN, one of America's most nimble formal poets, is the author of six collections, including three from Persea: *Straight Razor*, a finalist for the Lambda Literary Award; *Proprietary*, a finalist for the Northern California Book Award and the Lambda Literary Award; and *A Better Life*.

SARAH MATTHES is the author of *Town Crier* ("accessible and miraculous," according to *Brooklyn Rail*), a finalist for the National Jewish Book Award in poetry.

SHANE MCCRAE is one of the most innovative and important American poets writing today. His numerous acclaimed books include *The Animal Too Big to Kill*, which Persea published in 2015.

SANDRA MEEK is one of America's foremost ecological poets. Her six books include *Road Scatter*, *An Ecology of Elsewhere*, and *Still*, which was named a New & Noteworthy Book by the *New York Times Book Review*. She is the recipient of a Creative Writing Fellowship from the National Endowment for the Arts and the Lucille Medwick Memorial Award from the Poetry Society of America. She has been named Georgia Author of the Year in Poetry three times and twice received the Peace Corps Writers Award in Poetry.

THYLIAS MOSS is the author of many electrifying books, including *Last Chance for the Tarzan Holler* (a National Books Critics Circle Award finalist), *Slave Moth* (named by *Black Issues* as the Best Poetry Book of 2004), and *Wannabe Hoochie Mama Gallery of Realities' Red Dress Code: New & Selected Poems*, all published by Persea. She is the recipient of the Witter Bynner Prize, a National Endowment for the Arts grant, and fellowships from the MacArthur Foundation and the Guggenheim Foundation.

EDWARD NOBLES is the author of two collections of finely-honed poems: *Through One Tear* and *The Bluestone Walk.*

SUSANNAH NEVISON is the author of two collections of poetry, including *Teratology*, called "dynamic and beautifully hewn" by *Foreword Reviews*; and co-author, with Molly McCully Brown, of *In the Field Between Us*, a 2025 National Endowment for the Arts Big Read selection.

AMY NEWMAN is a poet and translator from the Italian. Her four ingenious poetry collections include *Dear Editor* and *On This Date in Poetry History*, described as "dazzling" in the *New York Times Book Review.*

KATE NORTHROP is the author of three uncanny collections, including *Clean* and *Things Are Disappearing Here*, named a New & Noteworthy Book by the *New York Times Book Review.*

JAMES RICHARDSON is a distinguished poet, aphorist, essayist, and literary critic. He is the recipient of the Jackson Poetry Prize, an Award in Literature from the American Academy of Arts and Letters, the Castagnola Prize from the Poetry Society of America, as well as fellowships from the National Endowment for the Humanities and the National Endowment for the Arts.

VALENCIA ROBIN, a poet and visual artist, is the author of *Ridiculous Light*—praised in the *San Francisco Chronicle* as "transcendent poems to give to your mother, your lover, your friends, yourself"—and *Lost Cities.*

PATRICK ROSAL is "one of the great poets of the Americas" (*El Paso Times*). His books (all from Persea) include *The Last Thing: New & Selected Poems*, winner of the William Carlos Williams Book Award from the Poetry Society of America, and *Brooklyn Antediluvian*, winner of the Lenore Marshall Prize from the Academy of American Poets.

CAREY SALERNO is the author of three gripping collections, including *Tributary* and *The Hungriest Stars*. She is Executive Director and Publisher of Alice James Books.

CHRISTOPHER SALERNO is the author of five books of poetry, including *The Man Grave*, a vulnerable and incisive exploration of contemporary American masculinity.

ALLISON SEAY is the author of *To See the Queen*, described in the *Colorado Review* as a book of "frightening, moving, deeply human poems."

LISA RUSS SPAAR is a decorated author, educator, critic, and novelist. Her most recent books are *Madrigalia: New & Selected Poems* and *Paradise Close*, a novel. She is the recipient of a Guggenheim Fellowship and the Library of Virginia Award for Poetry, among many other honors for her writing and teaching.

ALEXANDRA TEAGUE is a poet, novelist, memoirist, and a specialist in the oddities and perils of American culture, particularly of the American West and the Heartland. Her acclaimed poetry collections (all from Persea) include *[ominous music intensifying]*, *Or What We'll Call Desire*, *The Wise and Foolish Builders*, and *Mortal Geography*, which won the California Book Award Gold Medal for Poetry. She is the recipient of a National Endowment for the Arts Creative Writing Fellowship in Poetry, among other honors and distinctions.

EMILY VAN KLEY, poet and aerialist, is the author of *Arrhythmia* and *The Cold and the Rust*, a book that "explores Michigan's distinct topographies while attending to the intersections of rurality, whiteness, sexuality, and class" (*Harvard Review*).

SIDNEY WADE is a poet, translator, and birder, whose "imagination is as powerful as any American poet's since Wallace Stevens" (*Slate*). Her six delightful books of poetry include *Stroke* and *Straits & Narrows*.

SARA WAINSCOTT, a visionary sonneteer, is the author of *Insecurity Systems*.

RACHEL WETZSTEON (1967–2009) was a scholar and poet-flâneur. She wrote formally dexterous and delightful verse, much of it set in New York City, where she lived for most of her life. She wrote three books of poetry, including the posthumous *Silver Roses*, and a scholarly monograph on W. H. Auden. She was the poetry editor at the *New Republic*.

MICHAEL WHITE is the author of many admired books, including *Vermeer in Hell*, a collection of poems, and *Travels in Vermeer*, a memoir that was longlisted for the National Book Award.

CAKI WILKINSON is a poet and former star high-school point guard, the author of three nimble, wistful collections, including The *Wynona Stone Poems* and *The Survival Expo* (described in the *New York Times Book Review* as "delightful, clever, sometimes wrenching").

GARY YOUNG, writer and printmaker, is a master of the prose poem. His most recent books are *American Analects* and *That's What I Thought*. His honors include the Lucille Medwick Memorial Award, the Shelley Memorial Award, the William Carlos Williams Award, and the Lyric Poem Award, all from the Poetry Society of America; and grants from the National Endowment for the Arts, National Endowment for the Humanities, California Arts Council, and the Vogelstein Foundation. He was the inaugural Poet Laureate of Santa Cruz County.

Copyright Acknowledgments

Tom Andrews, "A Language of Hemophilia" (excerpt), from *The Brother's Country*, © 1990 by Tom Andrews, published by Persea Books

Jubi Arriola-Headley, "N'Jadaka's Appeal", from *Bound*, © 2024 by Jubi Arriola-Headley, published by Persea Books

Cameron Awkward-Rich, "Meditations in an Emergency," from *Dispatch*, © 2019 by Cameron Awkward-Rich, published by Persea Books

Aaron Belz, "Team", from *Glitter Bomb*, © 2014 by Aaron Belz, published by Persea Books

Paul Blackburn, "Ritual X: The Evening Pair of Ales", from *The Collected Poems of Paul Blackburn*, © 1955, 1960, 1961, 1966, 1967, 1968, 1969, 1970, 1971, 1972, 1975, 1978, 1980, 1983, 1985 by Joan Blackburn, reprinted by permission of Joan Blackburn

Elizabeth Bradfield, "In Preparation", from *Approaching Ice*, © 2010 Elizabeth Bradfield, published by Persea Books

Molly McCully Brown, "The Central Virginia Training Center", from *The Virginia State Colony for Epileptics and Feebleminded*, © 2017 by Molly McCully Brown, published by Persea Books

Gabrielle Calvocoressi, "She Ties My Bowtie", from *Rocket Fantastic*, © 1997 by Gabrielle Calvocoressi, published by Persea Books

Sarah Carson, "Ode to Flint, Michigan, Five Years, Three Months, Ten Days after the Water Crisis Began", from *How to Baptize a Child in Flint, Michigan*, © 2022 by Sarah Carson, published by Persea Books

Stacie Cassarino, "The Bats This Summer", from *Each Luminous Thing*, © 2023 by Stacie Cassarino, published by Persea Books

Paul Celan "Assisi", from *Poems of Paul Celan*, translation © 1972, 1980, 1999, 2002 by Michael Hamburger, published by Persea Books

Laura Cronk, "Marriage", from *Ghost Hour*, © 2020 by Laura Cronk, published by Persea Books

Aleš Debeljak, "A Bath Before Bed", from *Without Anesthesia: New and Selected Poems*, © 2011 by Aleš Debeljak, published by Persea Books

Tory Dent, "What Silence Equals," from *What Silence Equals*, © 1993 by Tory Dent, published by Persea Books, reprinted by permission of Sean Harvey

Mitchell L.H. Douglas, "Continuum", from *dying in the scarecrow's arms*, © 2018 by Mitchell L.H. Douglas, published by Persea Books

Rachel Galvin, "You Can Always Freeze Your Eggs," from *Uterotopia*, © 2022 by Rachel Galvin, published by Persea Books

Sarah Gambito, "I Am Not from the Phillipines", from *Loves You*, © 2019 by Sarah Gambito, published by Persea Books

Kimberly Grey, "A Difficult System", from *Systems for the Future of Feeling*, © 2020 by Kimberly Grey, published by Persea Books

Ramon Guthrie, "Today Is Friday", from *Maximum Security Ward and Other Poems*, © 1970, 1984 by Ramon Guthrie, published by Persea Books

Nazim Hikmet, "On Living", from *Poems of Nazim Hikmet*, translation © 1994, 2002 by Randy Blasing and Mutlu Konuk, published by Persea Books

Cynthia Marie Hoffman, "The Stork", from *Paper Doll Fetus*, © 2014 by Cynthia Marie Hoffman, published by Persea Books

Marie Howe, "Part of Eve's Discussion", from *The Good Thief*, © 1988 by Marie Howe, published by Persea Books

Kimberly Johnson, "Ode on My Episiotomy", from *Uncommon Prayer*, © 2014 by Kimberly Johnson, published by Persea Books

Shawn R. Jones, "Oomph," from *Date of Birth*, © 2023 by Shawn R. Jones, published by Persea Books

Wayne Koestenbaum, "Ode to Anna Moffo" (excerpt), from *Ode to Anna Moffo*, © 1990 Wayne Koestenbaum, published by Persea Books, reprinted by permission of the author

Anni Liu, "Xi'an Nocturne with Jasmine and Pears", from *Border Vista*, © 2022 by Anni Liu, published by Persea Books

Anne Marie Macari, "Black Line", from *Red Deer*, © 2015 by Anne Marie Macari, published by Persea Books

Osip Mandelstam, "[Take / for joy's sake / from these hands of mine]" from *Osip Mandelstam: 50 Poems*, translation © 1977 by Bernard Meares, published by Persea Books

Randall Mann, "Song", from *Straight Razor*, © 2013 by Randall Mann, published by Persea Books

Sarah Matthes, "What I Would Ask You", from *Town Crier*, © 2021 by Sarah Matthes, published by Persea Books

Sandra Meek, "Road Scatter", from *Road Scatter*, © 2012 by Sandra Meek, published by Persea Books

Thylias Moss, "Tornados" © 1991 by Thylias Moss, from *Rainbow Remnants in Rock Bottom Ghetto Sky*, published by Persea Books in 1991 and now included in *Wannabe Hoochie Mama's Gallery of Realities' Red Dress Code: New & Selected Poems*, published by Persea Books in 2016

Susannah Nevison, "Torsion", from *Teratology* © 2015 by Susannah Nevison, published by Persea Books

Amy Newman, "3 October", from *Dear Editor*, © 2011 by Amy Newman, published by Persea Books

Edward Nobles, "American Home," from *The Bluestone Walk*, © 2000 by Edward Nobles, published by Persea Books

Kate Northrop, "The Film", from *Clean*, © 2011 Kate Northrop, published by Persea Books

James Richardson, "Anyway", from *As If* © 1992 by James Richardson, published by Persea Books, reprinted by permission of the author

Valencia Robin, "Milwaukee, 1968", from *Ridiculous Light*, © 2019 by Valencia Robin, published by Persea Books

Patrick Rosal, "Children Walk on Chairs to Cross a Flooded Schoolyard", from *Brooklyn Antediluvian*, © 2016 by Patrick Rosal, published by Persea Books

Carey Salerno, "Invocation", from *Tributary*, © 2021 by Carey Salerno, published by Persea Books

Christopher Salerno, "Some History of Field Work", from *The Man Grave*, © 2021 by Christopher Salerno, published by Persea Books

Allison Seay, "Runaway Bride", from *To See the Queen*, © 2013 by Allison Seay, published by Persea Books

Lisa Russ Spaar, "New Year's Eve", from *Blue Venus*, © 2004 by Lisa Russ Spaar, published by Persea Books

Alexandra Teague, "Two Drafts Written After a Fight", from *Mortal Geography*, © 2010 by Alexandra Teague, published by Persea Books

Emily Van Kley, "Nonsomnolent", from *Arrhythmia*, © 2021 by Emily Van Kley, published by Persea Books

Sidney Wade, "O", from *Straights & Narrows*, © 2013 by Sidney Wade, published by Persea Books

Sara Wainscott, "[Cut buds bloom awhile in a water glass]", from *Insecurity System*, © 2020 by Sara Wainscott, published by Persea Books

Rachel Wetzteon, "Rain at Reading", from *Silver Roses*, © 2010 by Rachel Wetzsteon, published by Persea Books

Michael White, "Bioluminescence," from *Vermeer in Hell*, © 2014 by Michael White, published by Persea Books

Caki Wilkinson, "Jocks", from *The Survival Expo*, © 2021 by Caki Wilkinson, published by Persea Books

Gary Young, "[As the weather warms]", from *American Analects*, © 2024 by Gary Young, published by Persea Books